TREASURE BOOK

OF

Christmas Memories

H. JACKSON BROWN, JR.

ILLUSTRATIONS BY G.G. SANTIAGO

RUTLEDGE HILL PRESS®

Nashville, Tennessee

Published in Nashville, Tennessee, by Rutledge Hill
Press, Inc., 211 Seventh Avenue North, Nashville,
Tennessee 37219. Distributed in Canada by H. B. Fenn
and Co., Ltd., 34 Nixon Road, Bolton, Ontario L7E
1W2. Distributed in Australia by The Five Mile Press
Pty., 22 Summit Road, Noble Park, Victoria 3174.
Distributed in New Zealand by Southern Publishers
Group, 22 Burleigh Street, Grafton, Auckland.
Distributed in the United Kingdom by Verulam
Publishing, Ltd., 152a Park Street Lane, Park Street, St.
Albans, Hertfordshire AL2 2AU.

Typography by Compass Communications, Inc.,
Nashville, Tennessee.
Book design by Gore Studio, Inc., Nashville, Tennessee
ISBN: 1-55853-804-6
Printed in the United States of America.
1 2 3 4 5 6 7 8 9 — 04 03 02 01 00 99

INTRODUCTION

What a pleasure it was to contact people from all across the country and to ask them to share a favorite Christmas memory. Their heartwarming responses reminded me that no other holiday elicits so many poignant reminiscences and creates so many bright faces.

For Christmas is a time of joy, inspiration, and enduring traditions—the season for strengthening friendships and renewing faith.

It is my hope that this special collection of personal memories, poems, Bible verses, and excerpts from classics like Charles Dickens's *A Christmas Carol*, plus the charming illustrations by my friend G. G. Santiago, will help capture for you the magic and majesty of the Christmas season.

So bake the cookies, choose the tree, hang the wreath, sing the carols, and light the candles.

Memories to last a lifetime are just moments away.

HJB
Tall Pine Lodge
Fernvale, Tennessee

*P*eace on
earth begins with
peace in our home
and in
our heart.

A Christmas Memory

Before we opened our presents on Christmas Day, Grandfather would read the story "Yes, Virginia, There Is a Santa Claus" from a newspaper clipping that looked like it had been folded and refolded a thousand times. When he read it, everyone in the family, even the little ones, became quiet and attentive. It was a special moment that I looked forward to every year.

—Anna Elizabeth Robinson, age 35

Not believe in Santa Claus! You might as well not believe in fairies. . . . No Santa Claus? Thank God he lives and lives forever. A thousand years from now, Virginia, nay ten times ten thousand years from now, he will continue to make glad the heart of childhood.

—Frances Church,
"Yes, Virginia, There Is a Santa Claus"

FOR THE CHILDREN OR FOR THE GROWNUPS?

*T*is the week before Christmas and
  every night
  As soon as the children are
   snuggled up tight
And have sleepily murmured their
   wishes and prayers,
  Such fun does go on in the parlor
   downstairs!

For Father, Big Brother, and Grandfather, too,
  Start in with great vigor their
   youth to renew.
The grownups are having more fun
   than is said,
  And they'll play till it's long past
   their hour for bed.

They try to solve puzzles and each
      one enjoys
    The magical thrill of
      mechanical toys.
Even Mother must play with a doll
      that can talk
    And finds by assisting, it's able
      to walk.

It's really no matter if some paint may
      get scratched
    Or a wheel or a nut or a bolt
      gets detached.
The grownups are having such fun—
      all is well.
    The children don't know it, and
      Santa won't tell.

—Anonymous

A Christmas Memory

For the past ten years my sister and I have called several nursing homes the first week in December to get the names of ten or fifteen residents who don't receive much mail. We send each a beautiful Christmas card signed, "From your secret Santa."

—*Bryan Milsaps, age 31*

One night last winter when
the snow was deep
And sparkled on the lawn
And there was moonlight
everywhere,
I saw a little fawn.
I watched her playing in
the snow.
She did not want to leave.
She must have known before
she came
That it was Christmas Eve.

—*Marchette Chute*

THE
CHRISTMAS LETTER

I have a list of folks I know,
All written in a book,
And every year when Christmas comes,
I go and take a look.

And that is when I realize
That these names are more a part
Not only of the book they're in,
But of my very heart. . . .

For I am but a total
Of the many folks I've met.
And you are one of those
Whose love I'll ne'er forget.

And whether I have known you now
For many years or few,
In some way you have had a part
In shaping things I do.

And every year when Christmas comes,
I realize this anew:
The best gift life can offer me
Is meeting friends like you.

—Author Unknown

A Christmas Memory

We have a talent show in my family on Christmas Eve night. Each member of our family over the age of three must display some sort of talent using a Christmas carol. We have had everything from an interpretive dance of "Away in the Manger" to what "Silent Night" would be like if it were a painting. It's great family fun!

—*Keith Robinson, age 42*

A Christmas Memory

Every year I address and stamp all of my holiday cards and send them in a large manila envelope to the postmaster in Santa Claus, Indiana, or North Pole, New York. The postmaster adds a postmark from the town and mails them on. Friends love to receive cards from the North Pole or Santa Claus.

—*Sherese Van Miegham*

Mother always saw to it that we had a special outfit to wear on Christmas Day.

—*Annette Hayes, age 57*

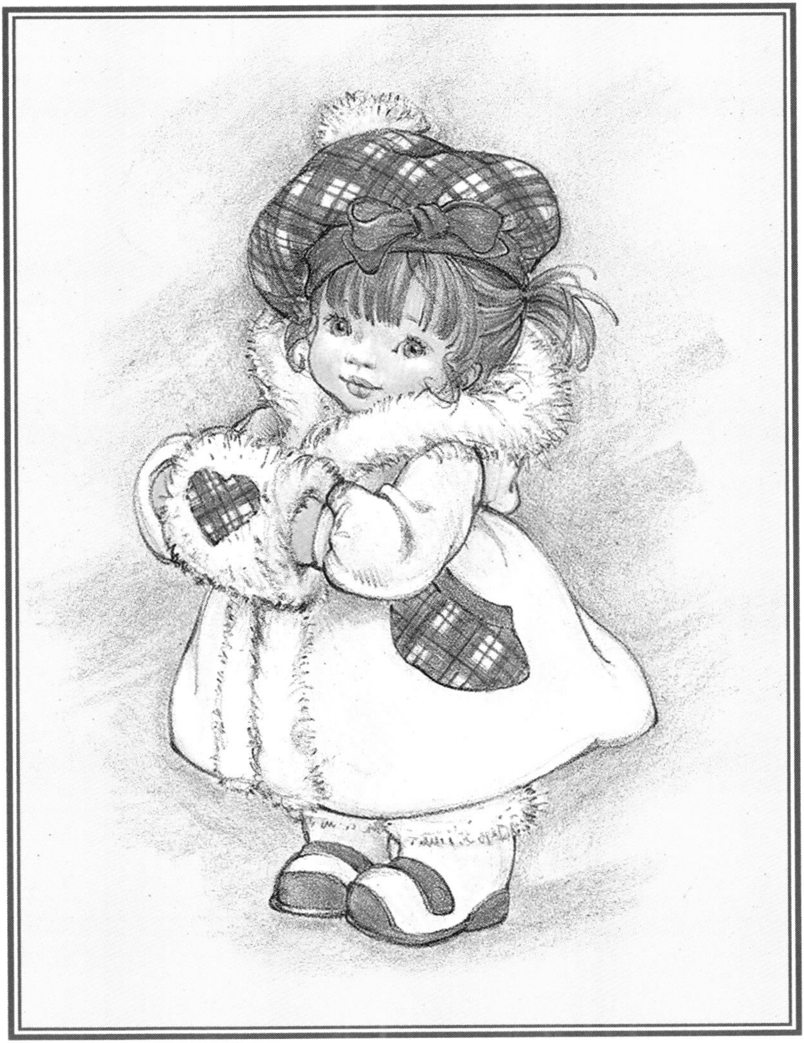

Don we now our gay apparel,

Fa la la, la la la, la la la.

Troll the ancient Yuletide carol,

Fa la la la la, la la la la.

—Traditional Welsh Carol

Scrooge dressed himself "all in his best," and at last got out into the streets. . . . He looked so irresistibly pleasant, in a word, that three or four good-humoured fellows said, "Good morning, sir! A merry Christmas to you!" And Scrooge said often afterwards, that, of all of the blithe sounds he had ever heard, those were the blithest in his ears.

—*Charles Dickens*, A Christmas Carol

A Christmas Memory

The first Christmas we were married, my new husband was overseas serving in World War II. I was all set to spend Christmas without him, when, lo and behold, who should come walking through the front door on Christmas morning—my husband! I was so surprised and excited! He had been wounded and was home to stay.

—Dorothy Bond, age 72

A Christmas Memory

I have three cats and two dogs. A few days before Christmas I buy them all festive matching Christmas collars with jingle bells. They all look so jaunty in their new collars!

—*Jeanie Young, age 52*

*Never select a
Christmas tree
after dark.*

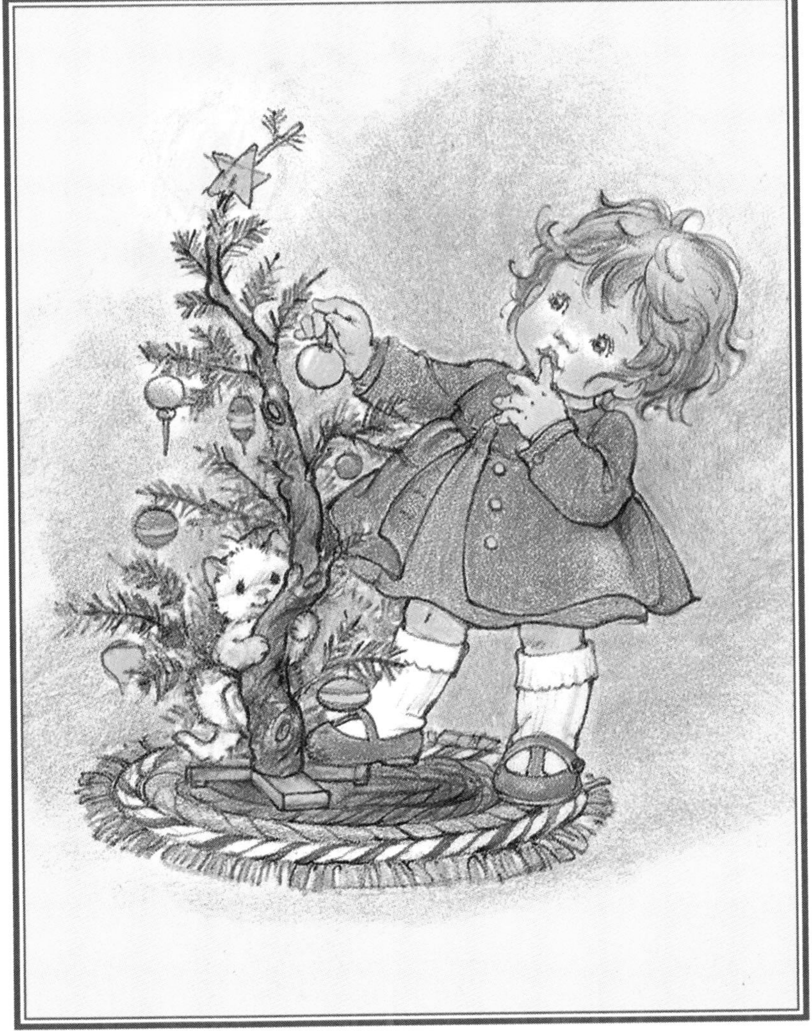

A Christmas Memory

We always picked out our Christmas tree on December 21, the date of the winter solstice. This reminded us that the Christmas tree is a symbol of life in the middle of winter, like the birth of Jesus.

—India Reynolds, age 33

In summer sun, or winter snow,
A dress of green you always show.
O Christmas tree, O Christmas tree,
With happiness we greet thee!

When decked with candles
once a year,
You fill our hearts with
Yuletide cheer.
O Christmas tree, O Christmas tree,
With happiness we greet thee!

—Traditional German Carol

A Christmas Memory

On Christmas Eve night my family formed a circle around the Christmas tree. Each of us held a lighted candle, and in total darkness, except for the tree lights and the candle lights, we sang "Silent Night" and "Away in a Manger."

—*Elizabeth Laine, age 80*

Dad cut a pine
From our back woods
Where it stood all heavy
with snow.
And we decorated it with lights
And tinsel trim
Till you couldn't see the tree
for the glow!

—*Anne Wood*

A Christmas Memory

Our father would always have a blazing fire going in the fireplace on Christmas Day. He would make a big deal of lighting it with a piece of the trunk saved from last year's Christmas tree.

—*Christine Blalock, age 45*

*E*verywhere, everywhere,
Christmas tonight!
Christmas in lands of the fir tree
and pine,
Christmas in lands of palm tree
and vine,
Christmas where children are
helpful and gay,
Christmas where old men are
patient and gray.
Everywhere, everywhere,
Christmas tonight!

—*Phillips Brooks*

A Christmas Memory

I use an old handmade red quilt as our Christmas tree skirt. It's always a special feeling when I get this treasured heirloom out of the cedar chest and spread it under the tree.

Another good idea is to create a Christmas tree skirt for your grown children made from their favorite clothes worn when they were growing up.

—*Roxienne Gill*

The holly is up,
The house is bright;
The tree is all ready,
The candles alight;
Rejoice and be glad
All children tonight.

—Old English Carol

A Christmas Memory

My favorite Christmas was the first one I spent with my husband. We had no money, no gifts, and a small, sad, "Charlie Brown" Christmas tree. We woke up Christmas morning, made breakfast together, and lit the few lights we had on our first and favorite tree.

—*Caroline Duncan, age 27*

A Christmas Memory

Before our kids went to bed on Christmas Eve we would read the poem "Twas the Night Before Christmas." We would all gather around the fireplace in our pajamas, and each of us would read a part of the poem. We would then go to bed as "visions of sugarplums danced in our heads."

—Joanne Gampher, age 65

Oh, how we loved to go caroling!

—*Amy Curtis, age 49*

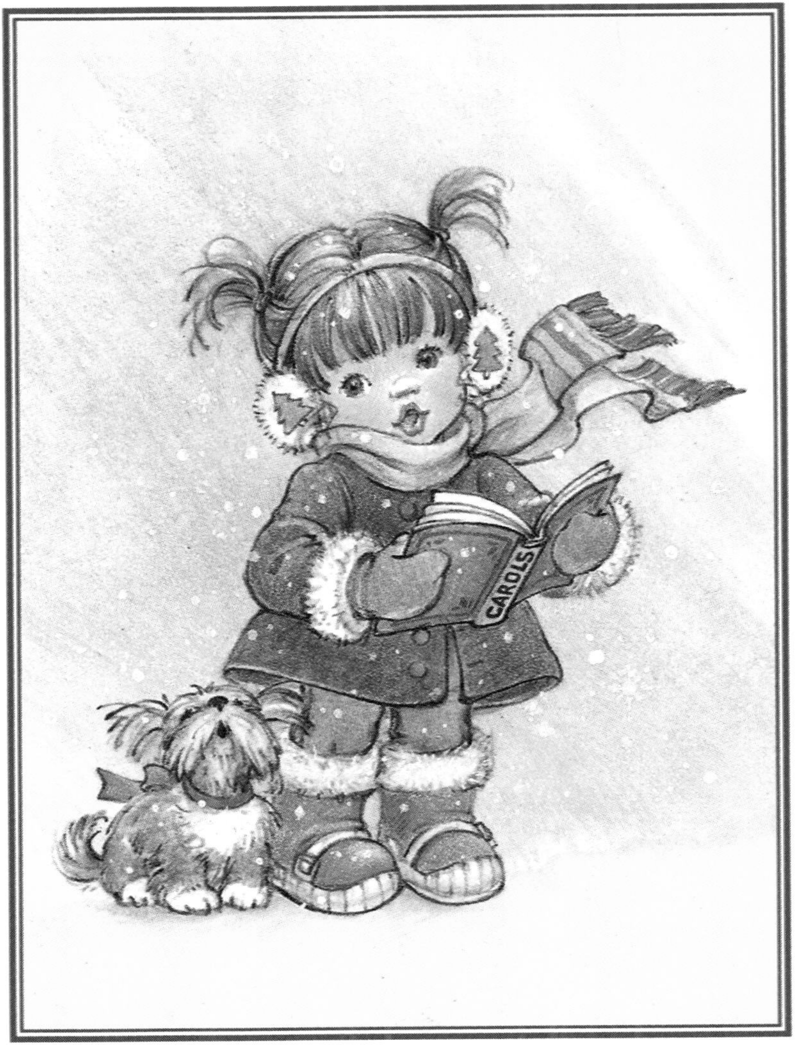
CAROLS

A Christmas Memory

We have a family tradition of going caroling two days before Christmas. When we return home, we always have the chili that my Mom has made and Christmas cookies that I have made.

—*Laura Coleman, age 18*

T wish," Scrooge muttered, putting his hand in his pocket, and looking about him, after drying his eyes with his cuff—"but it's too late now."

"What is the matter?" asked the Spirit.

"Nothing," said Scrooge. "Nothing. There was a boy singing a Christmas carol at my door last night. I should like to have given him something; that's all."

—Charles Dickens, A Christmas Carol

Here we come a-caroling
Among the leaves so green;
Here we come a-wand'ring,
So fair to be seen.
Love and joy come to you,
And to you glad Christmas too;
And God bless you and send you
A happy New Year,
And God send you a happy
New Year.

—*"Here We Come A-Caroling,"*
Traditional English Carol

A Christmas Memory

When I was a little girl, my daddy would hitch up the plow horses to a big sleigh with jingle bells on it. We lived in Vermont so there was usually snow on the ground. Daddy would guide our jingling sleigh into town where we would attend Christmas Eve services. Then we would jingle all the way home to wait for Santa.

—*Elizabeth Farcus, age 71*

*S*hepherds at the grange,
Where the Babe was born,
Sang with many a change,
Christmas carols until morn.

—*Henry Wadsworth Longfellow*

There's a song in the air!
There's a star in the sky!
There's a mother's deep prayer
And a baby's low cry!
And the star rains its fire
While the beautiful sing,
For the manger of Bethlehem
cradles a King.

—*Josiah Gilbert Holland*

A light shone from the window of a hut, and swiftly they advanced towards it. Passing through the wall of mud and stone, they found a cheerful company assembled round a glowing fire. An old, old man and woman, with their children and their children's children, and another generation beyond that, all decked out gaily in their holiday attire. The old man, in a voice that seldom rose above the howling of the wind upon the barren waste, was singing them a Christmas song—it had been a very old song when he was a boy—and from time to time they all joined the chorus.

—*Charles Dickens*, A Christmas Carol

O the snow, the beautiful snow,
Filling the sky and the
earth below.
Over the house tops, over
the streets
Over the heads of the people
we meet.
Dancing,
Flirting,
Skimming along,
Beautiful snow. It can do
nothing wrong.

—*John Whittaker Watson*

A Christmas Memory

My family has had the same poinsettia for fifteen years. It has become a very important symbol of hope and rebirth for us. We always put the poinsettia in the entry way so that it's the first thing all of our guests see. We have even named the red flower "Ruby." She is a very vital part of our Christmas tradition.

—*Maryanne Reynolds, age 70*

$\mathcal{A}$s fits the holy
Christmas birth,
Be this, good friend,
our carol still—
Be peace on earth,
be peace on earth,
To men of gentle will.

—*William Makepeace Thackery*

A Christmas Memory

Every Christmas, my mother set small, red glass boots on our mantle as decoration. On Christmas morning, I would find the boots filled with candy canes and peanuts. No matter what important gift I might have asked for that year, only when I saw those boots filled with nuts and candy did I know that Santa had come to see me. I don't remember the dolls or the toys I received, but I remember the red boots. Santa now fills these same boots for my own children.

—*Beth Wakefield, age 53*

*When you give
a big
Christmas hug,
be the last
to let go.*

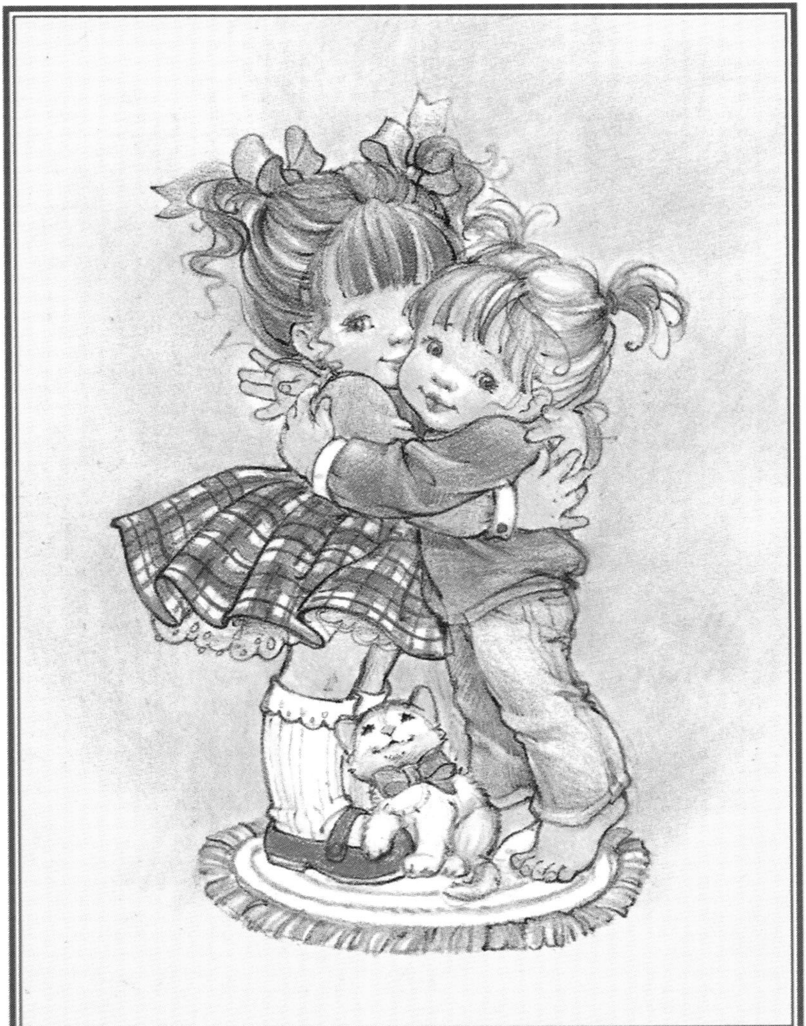

*W*hy, where's our Martha?"
cried Bob Cratchit looking round.
    "Not coming," said Mrs. Cratchit.
    "Not coming!" said Bob. . . .
"Not coming upon Christmas Day!"
    Martha didn't like to see him
disappointed, if it were only in joke;
so she came out prematurely from
behind the closet door and ran into
his arms. . . . And Bob . . . hugged
his daughter to his heart's content.

—*Charles Dickens*, A Christmas Carol

It is Christmas on
the highway,
in the thronging busy mart;
But the dearest,
truest Christmas
Is the Christmas in
your heart.

—Anonymous

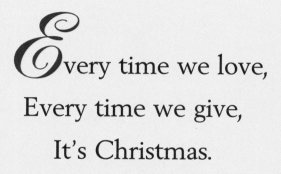

$\mathscr{E}$very time we love,

Every time we give,

It's Christmas.

—*Dale Evans Rogers*

A Christmas Memory

Before we open our gifts on Christmas morning, it is a tradition in our family for each of us to say what we are grateful for and to pray for people whom we are concerned about. It's a wonderful way to remember the true meaning of Christmas. Even the children enjoy this family custom.

—Robyn Blake, age 34

A Christmas Memory

When I was seven years old, my great-grandmother, who was in her nineties, took me outside on a snowy Christmas day. She lay down in the snow with me and together we made a snow angel family.

—*Millie Bartlett, age 47*

This is Christmas: not the tinsel, not the giving and receiving, not even the carols, but the humble heart that receives anew the wondrous gift, the Christ.

—Frank McKibben

A Christmas Memory

On December 10, our dad would always hang a Santa cap on the hall tree in our entryway. It let all of us kids know that Christmas was right around the corner.

—Sandi O'Neill, age 25

$\mathcal{T}$here's a wreath
on our door
tied with a big red bow
To welcome you, dear friend,
into our hearts and
out of the snow.

—*H. Jackson Brown, Jr.*

I try to have all my Christmas packages mailed by December 12th.

—JoEllen Gregg, age 61

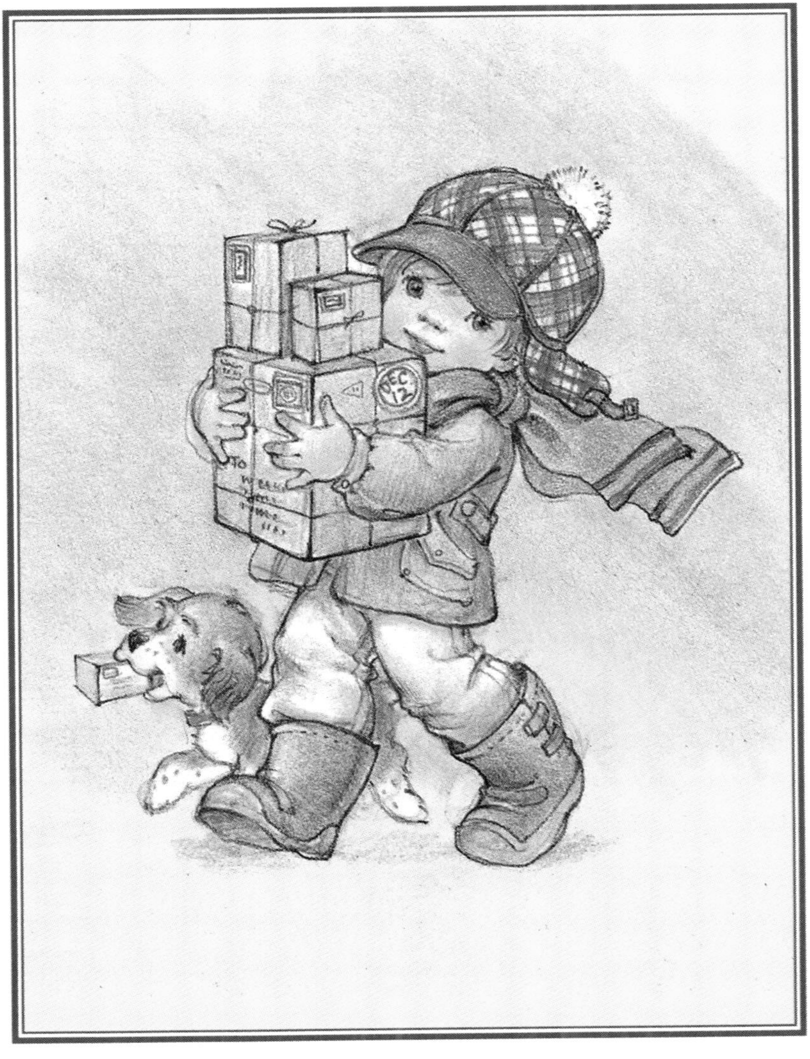
DEC 12
TO

A Christmas Memory

I'll never forget the Christmas that my grandmother got a tacky black bra. She put it on over her blouse and paraded around the room. Everyone agreed it was the funniest thing they had ever seen.

—Jill Jackson, age 17

Don't shake that package,
Don't peak 'neath the wrapping
for a better view.
And don't ask too many
questions;
It might be for you.

$\mathcal{G}$eorge Washington made this list of gifts that he wanted to give to his stepson and stepdaughter on Christmas Day, 1759:

A bird on Bellows

A Cuckoo

A turnabout Parrot

A Grocers Shop

An Aviary

A Prussian Dragon

A Man Smoakg

A Turnbridge Tea Set

3 Neat Turnbridge Toys

A Neat Book fash Tea Chest

A box best Household Stuff

A straw Patch box w. a Glass

A neat dress'd wax Baby

A Christmas Memory

Every year on Christmas morning I give all the young people in my family a silver dollar. I'm continuing a tradition my grandfather started. He always carried a lucky silver dollar in his pocket. My children, now all in their thirties and forties, have a wonderful collection of these lucky silver dollars that I've given them over the years.

—*Mike Young, age 59*

*Don't forget
whose birthday
we're celebrating.*

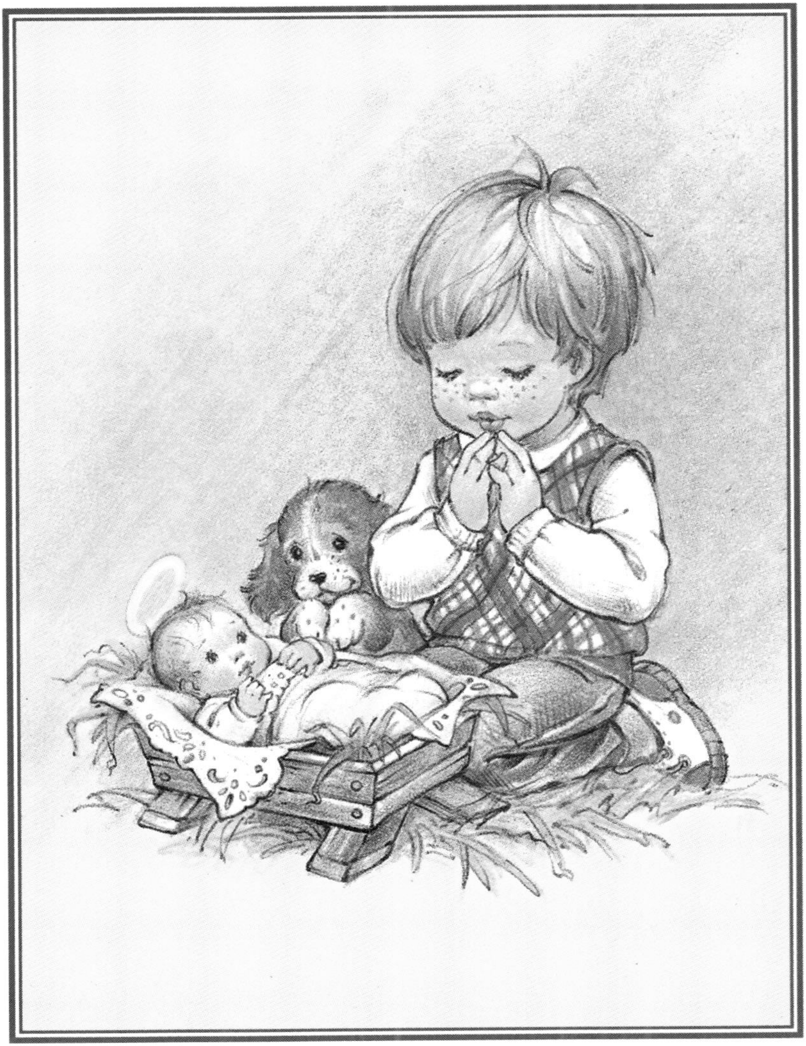

*G*o, tell it on the mountain,

Over the hills and everywhere;

Go, tell it on the mountain

That Jesus Christ is born!

—African-American spiritual

A Christmas Memory

As the youngest of four children I was given the privilege of placing the figure of the baby Jesus in the manger on Christmas morning. Then our father would read the Christmas story from the Book of Luke.

—Jennifer Crosby, age 31

And behold, the star which they had seen in the East went before them, till it came and stood over where the young Child was. When they saw the star, they rejoiced with exceeding great joy. And when they had come into the house, they saw the young Child with Mary His mother, and fell down and worshipped Him.

—*Matthew 2:9–11 (NKJV)*

A Christmas Memory

On Christmas Day my father followed an Old World tradition practiced by his great-grandparents of placing a handful of straw under the cloth on our dining room table. It was to remind us of Jesus' birth in the manger.

—*Jaye Weiner, age 34*

*C*andle, candle,
burning bright,
on our window sill tonight;
Like the shining Christmas star,
guiding shepherds from afar;
Lead some weary traveler here,
that he may share our
Christmas cheer.

—*Isabel Shaw*

Then let your heart be
filled with joy
While Christmas bells
are ringing,
And keep the birthday of
the Lord
With merriments and singing.

—*Mary Jane Carr*

For unto us a Child is born,

Unto us a Son is given;

And the government will be upon

His shoulder.

And his name will be called

Wonderful, Counselor,

Mighty God,

Everlasting Father, Prince of Peace.

—Isaiah 9:6 (NKJV)

The hinge of
history is on the
door of a
Bethlehem stable.

—*Ralph W. Sockman*

Don't count calories from December 15th through January 2nd.

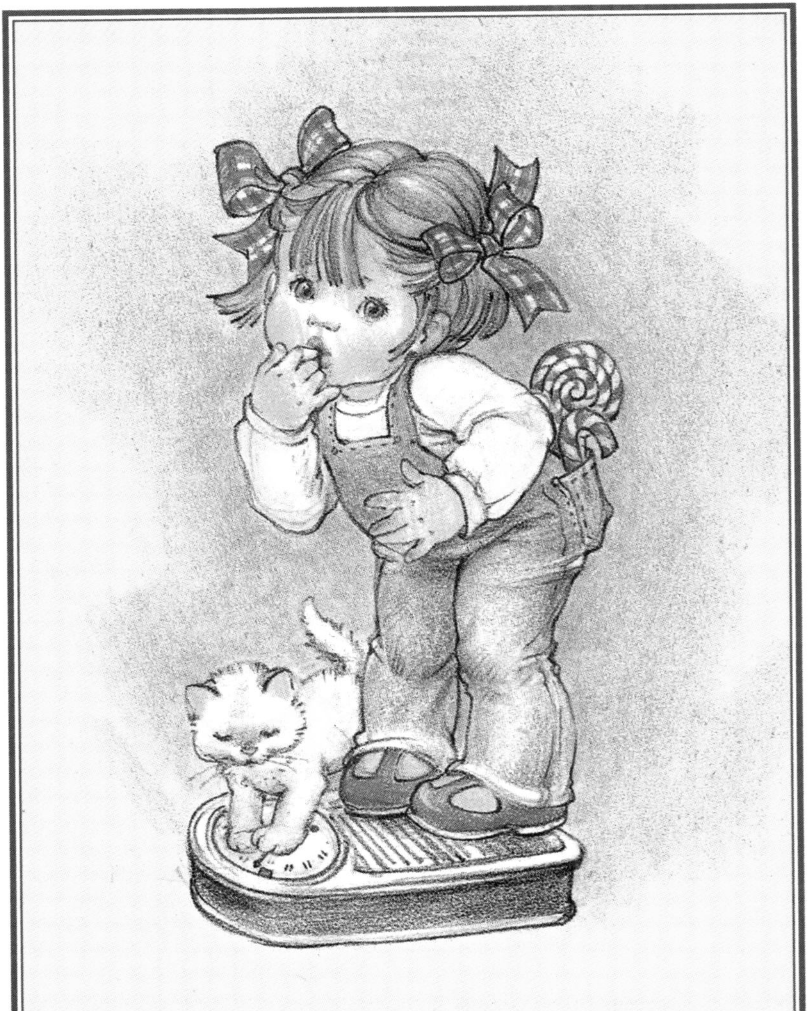

A Christmas Memory

On December 24th, our dad would visit the local bakery and buy the most scrumptious cinnamon coffee cakes. Then my sister and I would wrap them in cellophane and tie on big red bows. We joined Dad on Christmas morning as he made the rounds of the neighbors' houses, leaving a delicious coffee cake for them to enjoy as they opened their presents.

—*Fred Malone, age 73*

A Christmas Memory

For as long as I can remember, my family has gone to the same restaurant on Christmas Eve. When we get home, we take a family picture where the kids crowd around Mom and Dad who are seated in chairs in front of us. Then, we drink my mom's hot chocolate and eat Christmas cookies.

—Andrew Berg, age 24

*A*t Christmas be merry
and thank God of all,
And feast thy poor neighbors,
the great and the small.

—*Thomas Tusser*

A Christmas Memory

One of my favorite Christmas memories is our family's tradition of enjoying mini-Mars bars and tangerines on Christmas morning.

—*Marge Wilson, age 55*

*N*ow our neighbors'
chimneys smoke,
And Christmas logs are burning;
Their ovens with baked meats
do choke,
And all their spits are turning.
Without the day let sorrow lie,
And if for cold it hap to die,
We'll bury it in Christmas pie,
And evermore be merry!

—George Wither

A Christmas Memory

On the day before Christmas Eve, all the women in my family would gather in the kitchen at sunrise to start our Christmas bread. We would knead the bread and then wait for it to rise. We would talk about Christmas past and enjoy being together. By the end of the day we had forty loaves of bread that we would deliver to our friends and neighbors the next day.

—*Mavis Urban, age 62*

Mom had a special Christmas apron she wore only during the holidays.

—Irene Chapman, age 54

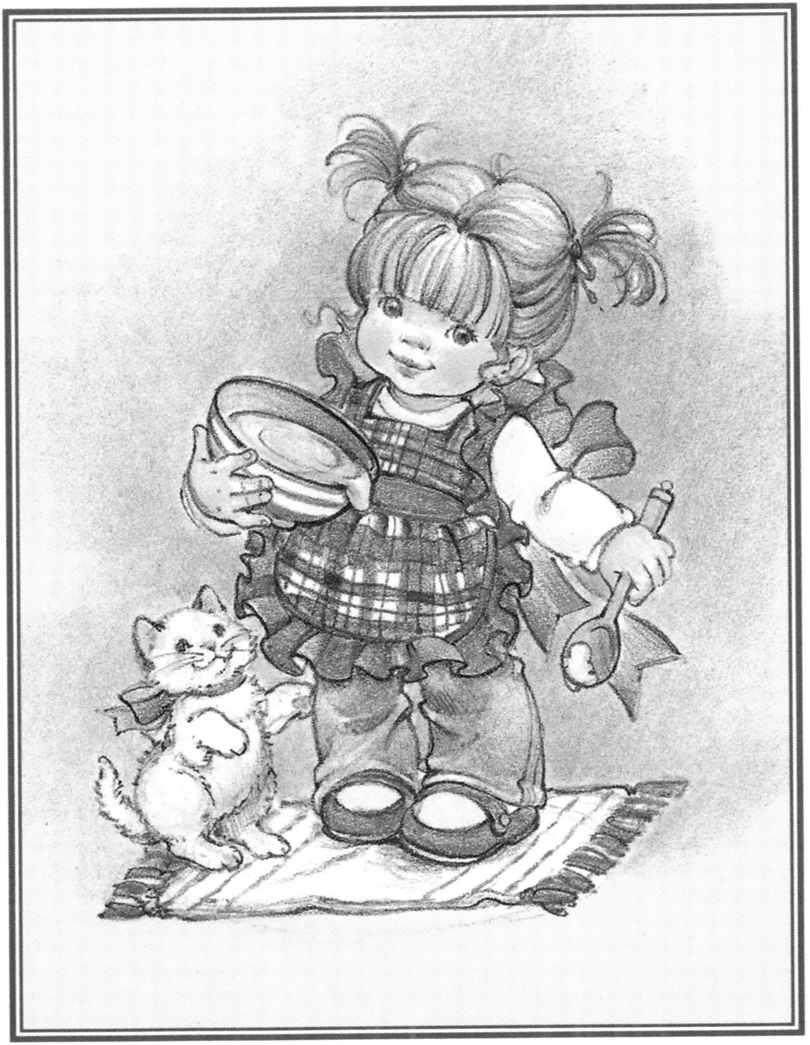

A Christmas Memory

We always make the same cookies that my grandmother made, and I plan to teach my children the same recipe. It's a great way to keep the tradition alive.

—*Jennie A. Daley, age 30*

*A*s many mince pies as
you taste at Christmas,
so many happy months
you will have.

—*Old English Saying*

For good luck throughout the coming year, sleep under a homemade quilt on Christmas Eve.

—*Sallie Bett Crowell, age 65*

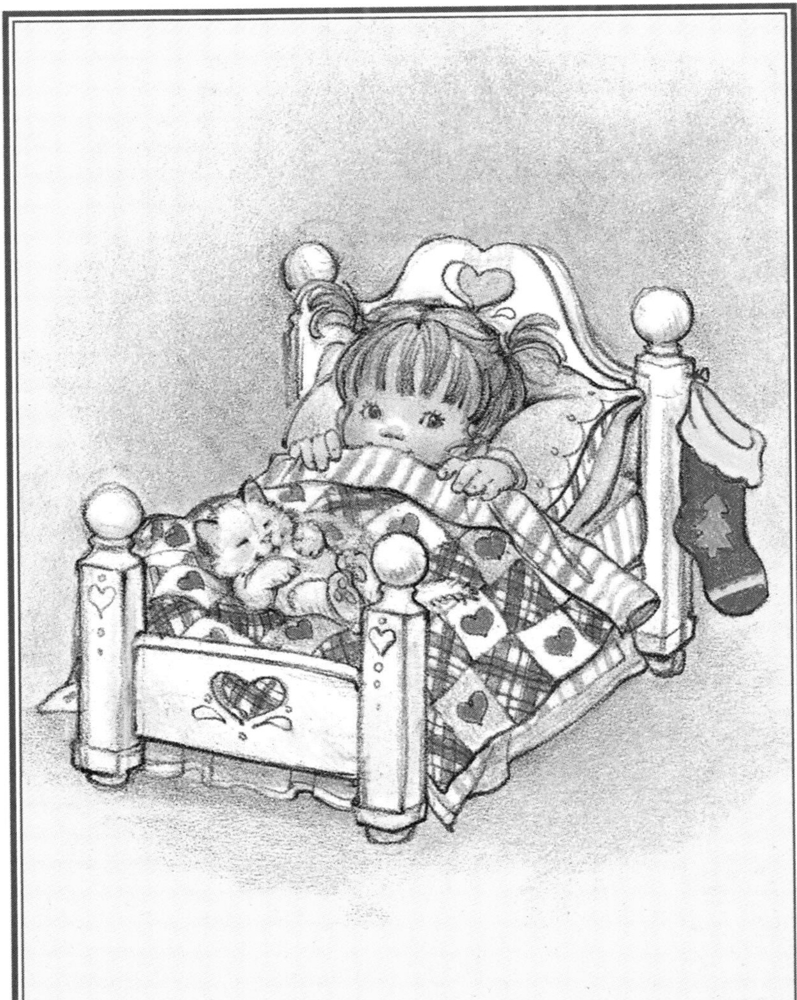

A Christmas Memory

Our neighborhood has its own parade with eight riding lawn mowers driven by dads wearing Santa hats. Kids decorate their bikes with garlands. Moms carry holiday flags and people put bows on their dogs. Santa rides in a pickup truck, and to top it off our volunteer fire department's big red truck serves as the parade's caboose.

—Sue Hines, age 38

don't know what to do!"
cried Scrooge, laughing and crying
in the same breath; and making a
perfect Laocoon of himself with his
stockings. "I am as light as a
feather, I am as happy as an
angel, I am as merry as a school-
boy. . . . A merry Christmas to
everybody! A happy New Year to
all the world!"

—*Charles Dickens,* A Christmas Carol

A Christmas Memory

When our kids were young, we would load everyone in the car on Christmas Eve with a thermos full of hot chocolate and blankets to snuggle up in and drive around town to look at all the Christmas lights. Hot chocolate, Bing Crosby on the radio singing Christmas songs, little children. It doesn't get much better!

—*Raino Aho, age 81*

Are you willing to believe that love is the strongest thing in the world—stronger than hate, stronger than evil, stronger than death—and that the blessed life which began in Bethlehem nineteen hundred years ago is the image and brightness of the Eternal Love? Then you can keep Christmas.

And if you keep it for a day, why not always?

—Henry van Dyke

*And don't forget
to take a walk
with someone
you love on
Christmas Day.*

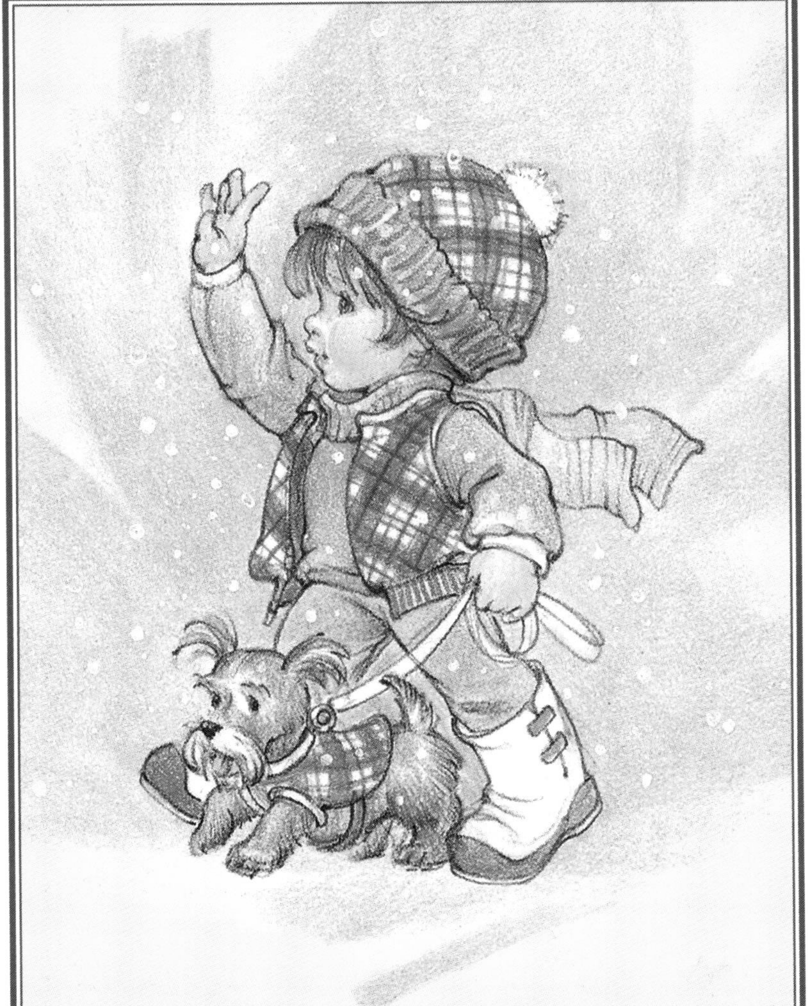

Dear Reader,

If you would like to share one of your favorite Christmas memories with me, I would love to hear from you.

My address is:

H. Jackson Brown, Jr.
P.O. Box 150014
Nashville, TN 37215

On the Web:
www.instructionbook.com
e-mail: llpio@aol.com